# Studying for a Driver's License

By Donald P. Joyce

Revised Review of Driver's Manual

Expanded Sample Questions and Definitions

Over 50 Illustrations

The Peoples Publishing Group, Inc.

# Foreword

This book is based on the New York state driver's manual. Where state driving laws may vary, provision is made for the reader to fill in his own state laws. Therefore, the reader should be alert to possible differences between the driving rules in this book and those in his own state's driver's manual.

Sections on traffic signs, traffic signals, and pavement markings are based on federal guidelines being adopted by the states, as described in the **Manual of Uniform Traffic Control Devices** by the New York State Department of Transportation. The same caution applies to these sections as well.

ISBN 0-88336-441-7

© 1985, First Edition 1973

The Peoples Publishing Group, Inc.
12 Overlook Avenue
Rochelle Park, NJ 07662



Printed in the United States of America

9   8   7

# Table of Contents


First, go over the state motor vehicle manual. Then study this review. You must know this Review of Driver's Manual very well in order to pass the test. If you find the reading too hard, have someone go over it with you.


Answering these questions will help you learn the Review of Driver's Manual.


Over 110 multiple choice questions just like the ones on the written driver's test you'll be taking.


Test yourself and get a score. Find out how you may do on a real test.


Answer keys for all 20 sample tests.


Hard words are simply defined.

# How to Use This Book

If you're studying to take the written test for your driver's license, then this book is for you!

**Studying for a Driver's License** explains driving rules in a way that is easy to understand. It also contains the signs, road markings, and signals that you'll need to study for your test. And it gives you a chance to practice answering test questions.

Step 1—Study a section of the Review of Driver's Manual. Some driving rules may differ from state to state. This book will tell you whenever this is the case. Then you should use your state manual to look up your state's rule. Also, be sure to look up any words you don't know.

Step 2—Answer the Review Questions that go with the section you studied. You may look back for help.

Step 3—Answer the Review Questions orally without looking back at the answers. If you can't, study the section some more.

Step 4—Do all the sections this way.

Step 5—Answer the Sample Questions. These questions are like the ones you'll find on the written test you'll take.

Step 6—Do the 20 Sample Tests.

# Review of Driver's Manual



## Drive to the right

1. Always drive to the right except:
   a. when preparing to make a left turn.
   b. when on a highway of more than two lanes where the right lane is for slow-moving traffic.
   c. when passing a vehicle.

2. Do not enter the opposing (left) lane when:
   a. approaching the crest (top) of a hill.
   b. approaching a curve.
   c. within 100 feet of a bridge.
   d. within 100 feet of railroad crossing.
   e. when pavement markings prohibit driving on the left.

## Passing other vehicles

1. When passing another vehicle always:
   a. look around to make sure it is safe to pass.
   b. signal that you are going to pass.
   c. be sure you have time and space enough to overtake the car ahead and return to the right lane before an approaching car comes within 200 feet of you.
   d. wait until you can see its front bumper in your rear view mirror before swinging back. On expressways, wait even longer.

2. Always pass on the left except:
   a. when the vehicle ahead is making a left turn.
   b. on a one-way street.
   c. on a road with two or more lanes in each direction.

3. Do not pass a stopped school bus. You may pass if waved on by the bus driver or a police officer.

4. Never pass a car when it has stopped at a crosswalk to allow a pedestrian to cross.

5. When you are passed, stay to your right, but don't go off the pavement, and slow down slightly.

# Right-of-way

1. The general rule is:

   At an intersection which has no traffic control device, the car on your right has the privilege of going first.

2. Exceptions to this rule are:

   a. A car already in the intersection has the right-of-way over a car preparing to enter.
   b. A car going straight ahead has the right-of-way over a car turning left.
   c. Fire engines, police, and ambulances have the right-of-way over all vehicles.
   d. Pedestrians in crosswalks have the right-of-way over all vehicles.
   e. A car entering a main road from a private road or driveway must yield the right-of-way.
   f. Vehicles already in a traffic circle have the right-of-way over those entering.

# Turning

1. When making a turn always:

   a. Look around to make sure it is safe.
   b. Reduce speed.
   c. Signal your intention to turn at least 100 feet before you reach the turn.
   d. On any left turn, if approaching traffic prevents turning immediately, move into the center of the intersection in your lane and wait for the traffic to clear.

2. U-turns are prohibited:

   a. near the crest of a hill.
   b. near curves.
   c. at an intersection.
   d. in any situation where drivers cannot see, or be seen, for a distance of at least 500 feet in either direction.

   **Note:** Laws regarding U-turns may be different in your state. Check your state manual for laws about U-turns.

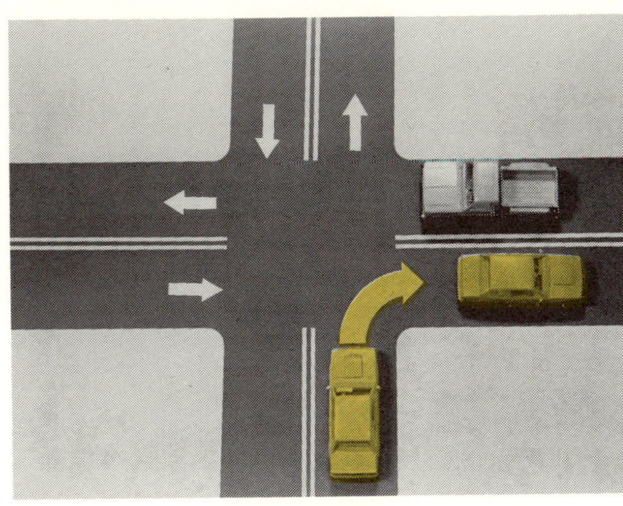

Figure 1

3. When making a right turn, keep as far right as possible. Make the turn as close as possible to the right curb or edge of the road. (See Figure 1).

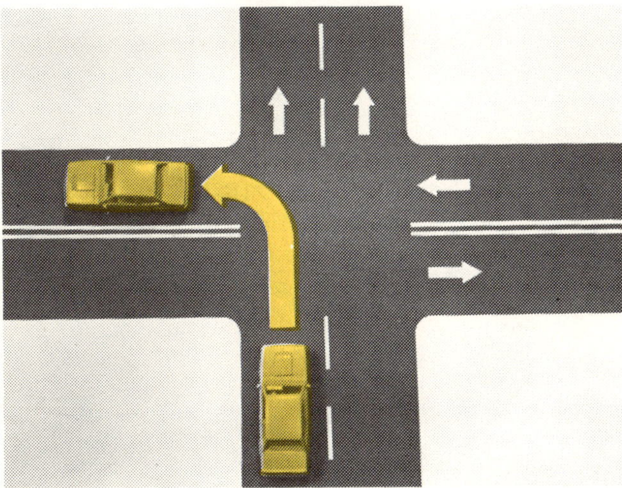

Figure 2

4. When making a left turn:

   a. from a one-way road onto a two-way road, approach the turn from the left lane. Make the turn to the left of the center of the intersection. (See Figure 2).

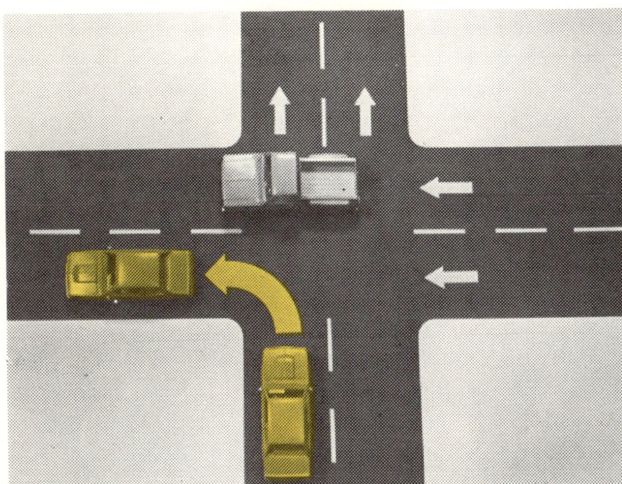

Figure 3

   b. from a one-way road onto another one-way road, approach the turn from the left lane. Make the turn as close as possible to the left curb or edge of the road. (See Figure 3).

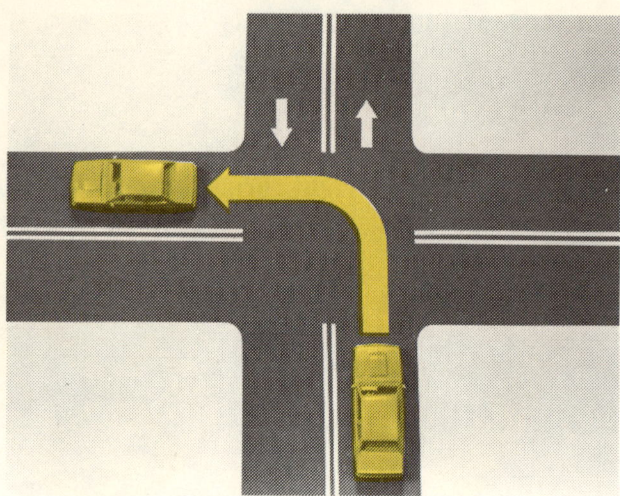

Figure 4

c. from a two-way road onto a two-way road, approach the intersection from as close as possible to the center line. Enter the intersection and then make the turn. (see Figure 4).

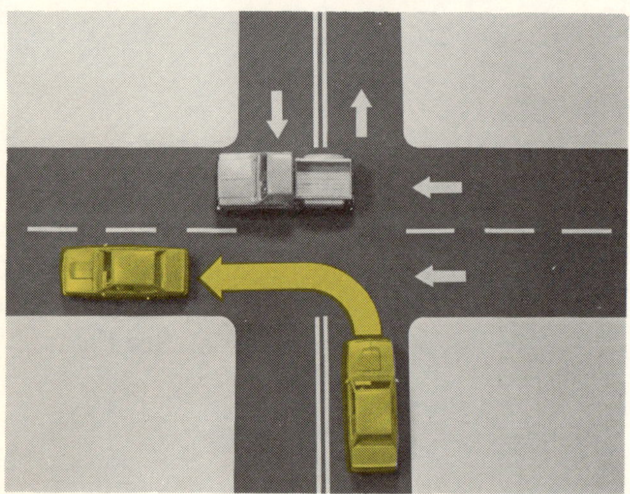

Figure 5

d. from a two-way road onto a one-way road, approach the turn from as close to the center line as possible. Make the turn before reaching the center of the intersection. (See Figure 5).

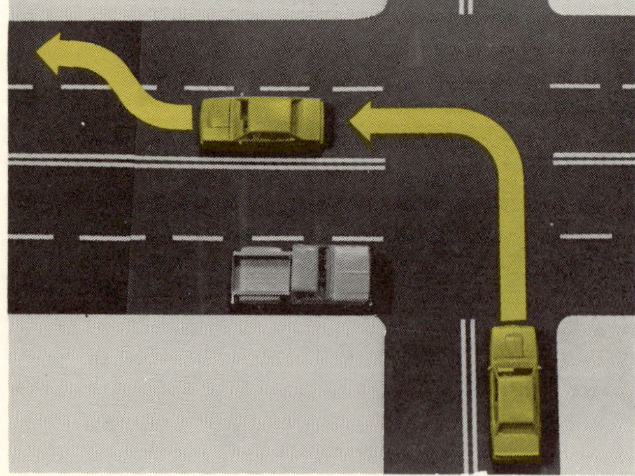

Figure 6

e. from a two-way road onto a four-lane highway, approach from as close as possible to the center line. Make the turn so that you enter the passing lane. When traffic permits, move to the right lane, out of the passing lane. (See Figure 6).

# Traffic signs

Figure 7

Figure 8

Figure 9

1. Figure 7 is a stop sign.
   a. It is an eight-sided sign. It has white letters on a red background.
   b. It tells you to come to a full stop and then proceed after yielding the right-of-way to others.
   c. Where to come to a full stop:
      (1) If there is a stop line, stop at the stop line.
      (2) If there is a crosswalk, stop before the crosswalk.
      (3) If there is no stop line and no crosswalk, stop near the intersection where you can see the traffic in both directions.

2. Figure 8 is a yield sign.
   a. It is a down-pointed triangle.
   b. It tells you to slow down and get ready to stop if necessary. Give the right-of-way to vehicles and pedestrians. It is the same as a stop sign except that you do not have to come to a full stop unless necessary.

3. Figure 9 is a railroad crossing sign.
   a. It is a round, yellow sign with a black **X** and lettering.
   b. It warns that you are approaching a railroad crossing. You should be prepared to slow down or stop. If you are following a bus or truck, you should know that some are required to stop at railroad crossings.

| Figure 10 | Figure 11 | Figure 12 | Figure 13 |

4. Regulatory signs regulate, or tell what the rules are.

   a. They are rectangular signs with black letters on a white background, or square white signs with a black symbol covered by a red circle and slash. The red circle means that you are not allowed to do what the symbol shows.

   b. Figure 10 tells you there is no left turn.

   c. Figure 11 tells you that you may not make a U-turn.

   d. Figure 12 tells you that you are going the wrong way on a one-way road.

   e. Figure 13 tells you to keep to the right.

   **Note:** Look in your state manual for other examples of regulatory signs.

| Figure 14 | Figure 15 | Figure 16 |

5. Warning signs warn you of something.

   a. Warning signs are diamond-shaped. They have black letters or symbols on a yellow background. (School and school crossing signs are five-sided.)

   b. Figure 14 warns you that a curve is ahead. The direction of the arrow tells you the direction of the curve. You should be prepared to slow down.

   c. Figure 15 warns you that a traffic signal is ahead. You should be prepared to stop if necessary.

   d. Figure 16 warns you of merging traffic. You should be alert for traffic that may be merging with your lane.

Figure 17

Figure 18

Figure 19

e. Figure 17 warns you that you are nearing a school crossing. You should be prepared to slow down and possibly stop for school buses or children crossing.

f. Figure 18 warns you that the road surface becomes slippery when wet. If it is raining or the road surface looks wet, you should be prepared to reduce your speed.

g. Figure 19 warns you that an intersection is ahead. You should be alert for traffic that may be turning into your lane. If you plan on making a turn at the intersection, you should make sure you are in the correct lane from which to make the turn.

**Note:** Look in your state manual for other examples of warning signs.

Figure 20

Figure 21

Figure 22

Figure 23

6. Guide signs tell you where you are.

a. Destination signs are rectangular, green signs with white lettering. They tell the distances to towns and cities. (See Figure 20).

b. Many roads are numbered with route markers. Route markers come in different shapes and colors.

(1) Figure 21 tells you what U.S. route you're on.
(2) Figure 22 tells you what interstate you're on.
(3) Figure 23 tells you what state route you're on.

**Note:** Look in your state manual for other examples of guide signs.

# Traffic signals

Figure 24

Figure 25

Figure 26

Figure 27

1. Traffic signals direct the flow of traffic.

   a. A steady red alone or a steady red arrow means to stop and wait for a green light or arrow. (See Figure 24).

   b. A steady yellow alone or a steady yellow arrow warns you the red light will follow. Do not enter the intersection after the red light comes on. (See Figure 25).

   c. A steady green alone means you may proceed through the intersection or make a turn, unless a sign prohibits the turn. However, you must yield to any vehicles and pedestrians in the intersection when the light changes green. (See Figure 26).

   d. A steady green arrow means move in the direction of the arrow, but give the right-of-way to pedestrians or traffic within the crosswalk or intersection. (See Figure 27).

   e. A flashing red light means the same as a stop sign.

   f. A flashing yellow light means to proceed with caution.

   g. Whenever you see a traffic officer obey his directions over all signals and signs.

# Pavement markings

Figure 28

Figure 29

Figure 30

Figure 31

Figure 32

Figure 33



1. White lines separate lanes of traffic moving in the same direction.

   a. A single, broken, white line defines traffic moving in the same direction. You may cross it if crossing will not interfere with traffic. (See Figure 28).

   b. A single, solid, white line is a warning line. You should stay in the lane, but you may cross if traffic conditions are OK. (See Figure 29).

2. Yellow lines separate lanes of traffic moving in opposite directions.

   a. A single, broken, yellow line defines traffic lanes moving in opposite directions. You may cross it if crossing will not interfere with traffic. (See Figure 30).

   b. A single, solid, yellow line and a broken, yellow line means you may cross it, if the broken line is on your side. If the solid line is on your side, you many not cross it except to make a left turn into or out of a driveway or alley. (See Figure 31).

   c. A double, solid, yellow line means you can't cross in either direction except to make a left turn into or out of a driveway or alley. (See Figure 32).

3. A diagonal line shows a change in pavement width or the number of lanes. Diagonal lines may be white or yellow. If the solid line at the edge of the road moves in, it means the highway gets narrower. (See Figure 33).

# Parking

Figure 34

Figure 35

Figure 36

1. Figure 34 shows a no stopping sign. It means you may not stop for any purpose, except when directed to by a police officer.

2. Figure 35 shows a no standing sign. It means you may stop only temporarily to receive or discharge passengers.

3. Figure 36 shows a no parking sign. It means you may stop only temporarily to load or unload merchandise or passengers.

4. The following are some parking regulations.
   a. There is no stopping, standing or parking:
      (1) on a sidewalk.
      (2) within an intersection.
      (3) on a bridge.
      (4) on a crosswalk.
      (5) on railroad tracks.
   b. There is no standing or parking:
      (1) in front of a driveway.
      (2) within 20 feet of a crosswalk at an intersection.
   c. There is no parking:
      (1) within 15 feet of a fire hydrant, except when a licensed driver, who can move the vehicle, is inside.

      **Note:** The number of feet may be different in your state. If it is, cross out the rule above, fill in the right number in the rule below and use that rule from now on.

      Within _________ feet of a fire hydrant.
      (2) on the road side of parked vehicle (double parking).

5. These are some guidelines for parking:
   a. When parking, you must park within 12 inches of the curb.

      **Note:** The number of inches may be different in your state. If it is, cross out the rule above, fill in the right number in the rule below, and use that rule from now on.

      You must park within _________ inches of the curb.
   b. When parking between two cars, allow enough space at both ends of your vehicle.

# Backing up

1. When backing up:
   a. Check mirrors and then turn your head to make sure the way is clear.
   b. Get out and walk to the back, if there is any chance a child is behind the car.

2. Never back up onto an open highway or expressway.

# Pedestrians

1. Always walk on the side of the road facing oncoming traffic if there are no sidewalks.

2. A blind person always has the right-of-way when crossing the street with a white or metallic cane, or when accompanied by a seeing-eye dog.

# Defensive driving

1. This means anticipating errors by others and being ready to react to the mistakes of others.

2. Expect the other driver to do the wrong thing.

# Speed and following distances

1. Federal law sets the maximum speed at 65. However, states can post lower speed limits.

2. Sometimes, minimum speeds are given. This means you may not go slower than the minimum speed. Minimum speeds are used to keep traffic moving smoothly.

3. The rule for following distance is one car length for each 10 miles per hour of speed.
   a. For example, the following distance is three car lengths at 30 miles per hour.
   b. At 60 miles per hour the following distance is six car lengths.

4. Travel at a speed that allows you to keep control of your vehicle at all times. When selecting a speed to travel at, consider:

   a. the flow of traffic. Cars that lag behind or speed ahead interrupt the flow of traffic and create dangerous situations.
   b. your ability to see ahead of you. You should always be able to stop your vehicle within the area you can see ahead of your car. Always reduce speed when vision is limited.
   c. the condition of the highway.
   d. the condition of your vehicle.
   e. your physical condition.

## Vehicle condition

1. Steering

   Vehicle should not pull to one side or vibrate.

2. Tires

   All tires must have at least 2/32 of an inch of tread.

3. Brakes

   a. If the car pulls to one side, the brakes need adjusting.
   b. The law says that brakes must stop a car within 30 feet at 20 miles per hour.

      **Note:** The number of feet may be different in your state. If it is, cross out the rule above, fill in the right number in the rule below, and use that rule from now on.

   The law says that brakes must stop a car within ___________ feet at 20 miles per hour.

## Driver's physical condition

1. Fatigue

   If you get drowsy: rest, open the window, stop and get out of the car and walk.

2. Alcohol

   a. As a general rule, drinking and driving do not mix. Whenever possible, do not drink and drive.
   b. Alcohol impairs your vision, interferes with your control, slows down your reflexes, and impairs your judgment.
   c. If you do drink and drive, know your limit. How much is safe to drink is not the same for everyone. Key factors are weight, time, and amount.
   d. Things you can do to control the effects of drinking are:
      (1) Eat some food before you drink and while you drink.
      (2) Limit yourself to one drink per hour.
      (3) Set a limit for yourself and then stick to it.

e. Drinking and driving laws have become tougher. Any or all of the following could happen if you are convicted of drunk driving (driving while intoxicated).

   (1) You can be fined.
   (2) You can be sent to jail.
   (3) You can be ordered to attend a driver education program.
   (4) Your license can be suspended.
   (5) Your license can be revoked.

**Note:** Check your state's driver's manual to find out what the penalty for drinking and driving is in your state.

3. Other drugs and medicines

a. Many other drugs besides alcohol can make you an unsafe driver. They include drugs a doctor prescribes; drug-store medicines like cough syrup, allergy pills, or cold pills; and illegal drugs.

b. Whenever a doctor prescribes a drug for you, ask about the effect it may have on your driving. Read labels on drug-store medicines carefully.

c. Many states have also toughened their laws regarding driving under the influence of drugs. Check your state manual to find out what the law is in your state.

## Safety precautions

1. Every driver is responsible for driving in a safe manner. Some safety precautions that all drivers should take are:

a. Always make sure headlights are clean and operating properly. This is especially important for night driving.

b. Make sure the windows are clean and nothing in the front or rear of the car is obstructing your view.

c. Adjust all mirrors — inside and out.

d. Use your seat belt. In 1984, New York passed a law requiring all drivers and passengers in the front seat to wear seat belts. Check your state's manual to find out if your state has such a law or is considering one.

2. In many states, the law requires that young children riding in a car be placed in an approved child safety seat. Check your state's manual to find out if your state has such a law. If so, fill out the rule below.

All children under the age of _______ must be transported in a child restraint seat.

# Expressway driving

1. Expressway driving is different from ordinary driving. You must think faster and handle your vehicle more effectively at higher legal speeds.

2. The acceleration lane is used to enter an expressway. It is where you accelerate (speed up) to cruising speed before merging with traffic.

3. The deceleration lane is used to leave the expressway. It is where you slow down before merging with slower traffic.

4. Some tips on expressway driving are:
   a. Stop and rest on long trips.
   b. Keep a window open.
   c. Wear good sunglasses on bright days.
   d. Never wear sunglasses at night.

5. If your vehicle should break down:
   a. Get completely off the pavement.
   b. Turn on the emergency warning lights or parking lights.
   c. Use color-coded balloons or put cloth on the door handle or antenna.

# Special driving conditions

1. Night driving is very dangerous because the amount we see is greatly reduced.
   a. You must use headlights, not parking lights, when it's dark.
   b. You must drop your headlights to low beam when you are within 500 feet of an approaching vehicle or 200 feet of a vehicle that you are following.

   **Note:** The number of feet may be different in your state. If it is, cross out the rule above, fill in the right number in the rule below, and use that rule from now on.

   You must drop your headlights to low beam when you are within 500 feet of an approaching vehicle or _______ feet of a vehicle that you are following.

2. Winter driving means a greater chance of emergency conditions.
   a. If you start to skid, do not brake or abruptly decelerate. Steer gently into the skid.
   b. Snow tires or chains must be used on snow emergency streets.

3. In fog or mist, put headlights on low beam, never on high beam.

# Handling driving emergencies

1. There is one basic rule: Think before you act. This applies to all driving situations and especially in emergency situations.

2. If you have a blowout, hold tightly to the steering wheel and ease up on the gas. Don't brake.

3. If you lose a wheel, react the same as for a blowout.

4. If your brakes fail, try pumping the brake pedal. Use the emergency brake or parking brake.

5. If you run off the pavement, don't try to swerve back on the pavement. You may throw your car off balance. Stay on the shoulder and ease up on the gas.

6. If a car is approaching you in your lane, pull to the right, slow down, use your horn, and flash your lights. Do not turn into his lane.

# If you are involved in an accident

1. If you are involved in an accident:
   a. Stop immediately at the scene.
   b. Give your name, address, license number, and registration number to the other driver, and get the same from him.

2. An accident must be reported to the state:
   a. if it involves death or personal injury.
   b. if it involves property damage over $400.

   **Note:** This amount may be different in your state. If it is, cross out the rule above, fill in the right number in the rule below, and use that rule from now on.

   If it involves property damage over $ ________ .

3. You must make the report within 10 days after the accident.

   **Note:** The number of days may be different in your state. If it is, cross out the rule above, fill in the right number in the rule below, and use that rule from now on.

   You must make the report within ______ days after the accident.

# Review Questions

## Drive to the right

1.  Give three exceptions to the rule "drive to the right."

    a. _________________________________________________

    ___________________________________________________

    b. _________________________________________________

    ___________________________________________________

    c. _________________________________________________

    ___________________________________________________

2.  When may you not enter the opposing lane?   Give five examples.

    a. _________________________________________________

    b. _________________________________________________

    c. _________________________________________________

    d. _________________________________________________

    e. _________________________________________________

## Passing other vehicles

3.  In order to pass another vehicle safely, what is the minimum number of feet there should be between you and an oncoming car after you complete the pass? __________

4.  After passing a car, when can you swing back? ___________________________

    ___________________________________________________

5.  Give three exceptions to the rule "pass on the left."

    a. _________________________________________________

    ___________________________________________________

    b. _________________________________________________

    ___________________________________________________

c. _______________________________________

_______________________________________

6. Give the exception to the rule "do not pass a stopped school bus."

_______________________________________

_______________________________________

7. May you ever pass a car when it has stopped at a crosswalk to allow a pedestrian to cross?

_______________________________________

8. What should you do when you are passed? _______________________

_______________________________________

_______________________________________



## Right-of-way

9. What is the general rule regarding right-of-way at an intersection which has no traffic control device?

_______________________________________

_______________________________________

10. Explain these exceptions to the general rule regarding right-of-way.

a. A car already in an intersection _______________________

_______________________________________

b. A car going straight ahead _______________________

_______________________________________

c. Emergency vehicles _______________________

_______________________________________

d. Pedestrians in crosswalks _______________________

_______________________________________

e. A car entering a main road from a private road _______________________

_______________________________________

f. Vehicles already in a traffic circle _______________________

_______________________________________

# Turning

11. At least how many feet before making a turn must you signal your intention of doing so?

    _______________________________________________________________

12. If approaching traffic prevents your making a left turn immediately, what should you do?

    _______________________________________________________________

    _______________________________________________________________

13. Where are U-turns prohibited?

    a. ____________________________________________________________

    b. ____________________________________________________________

    c. ____________________________________________________________

    d. ____________________________________________________________

14. When making a right turn, where should your vehicle be?

    _______________________________________________________________

    _______________________________________________________________

    Draw an arrow in Figure 37 to show this.

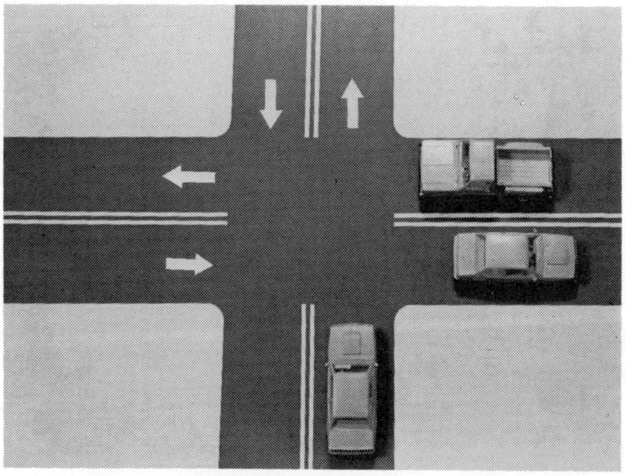

Figure 37

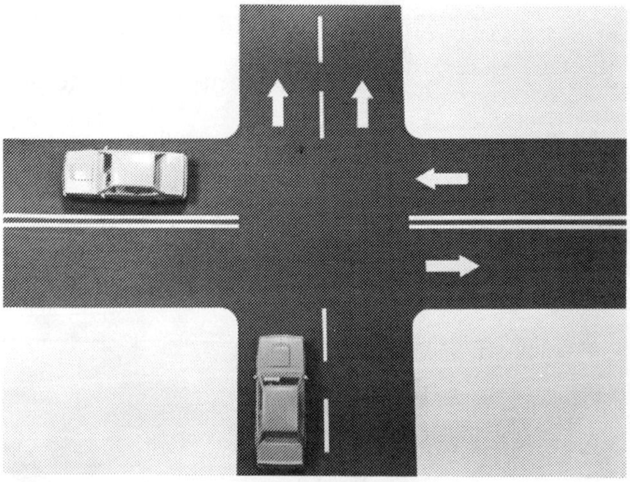

Figure 38

15. When making a left turn from a one-way road onto a two-way road, where should you make the turn?

    _______________________________________________________________

    _______________________________________________________________

    Draw an arrow in Figure 38 to show this.

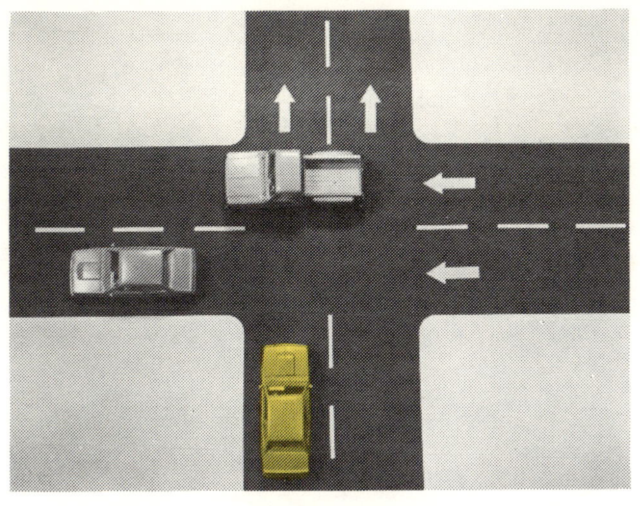

Figure 39

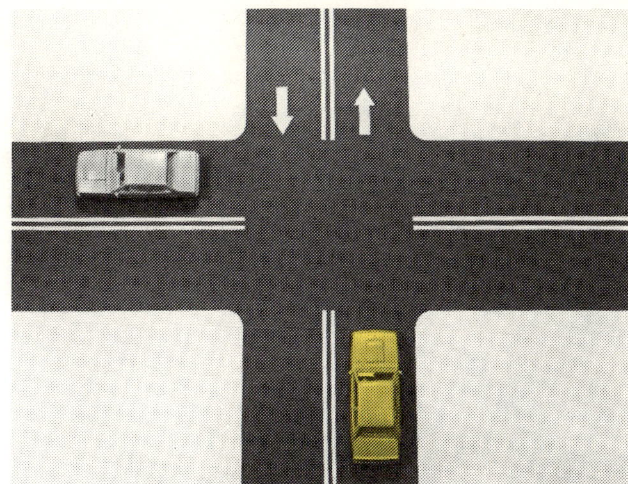

Figure 40



16. When making a turn from a one-way road onto another one-way road, where should you make the turn?

______________________________________________

______________________________________________

Draw an arrow in Figure 39 to show this.


17. When making a left turn from a two-way road onto another two-way road, where should you make the turn?

______________________________________________

______________________________________________

Draw an arrow in Figure 40 to show this.

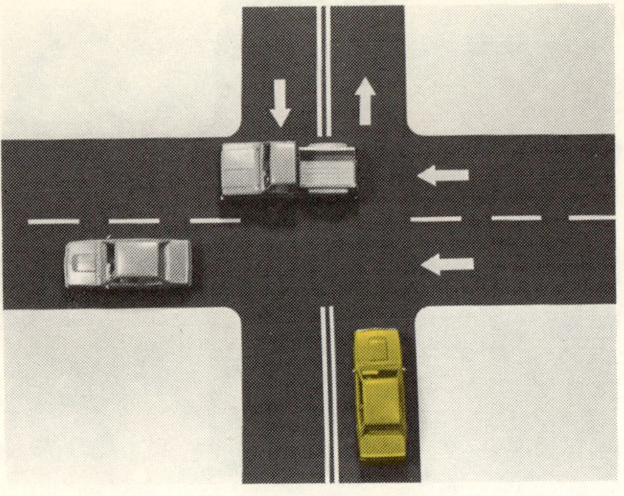

<table>
<tr><td>Figure 41</td><td>Figure 42</td></tr>
</table>

18. When making a turn from a two-way road onto a one-way road, where should you make the turn?

_________________________________________________

_________________________________________________

Draw an arrow in Figure 41 to show this.

19. When making a left turn from a two-way road onto a four-lane highway, which lane should you turn into?

_________________________________________________

_________________________________________________

Draw an arrow in Figure 42 to show this.

## Traffic signs

Figure 43

20. What does the sign in Figure 43 tell you? _______________________

_________________________________________________

_________________________________________________

21. If there is a stop line at an intersection with a stop sign, where must you stop?

_______________________________________________________________________

_______________________________________________________________________

22. If there is a crosswalk at an intersection with a stop sign, where must you stop?

_______________________________________________________________________

_______________________________________________________________________

23. If there is no stop line and no crosswalk at an intersection with a stop sign, where must you stop?

_______________________________________________________________________

_______________________________________________________________________

Figure 44                    Figure 45

24. What does the sign in Figure 44 tell you? ___________________________

_______________________________________________________________________

_______________________________________________________________________

25. In what way is a yield sign not like a stop sign? ____________________

_______________________________________________________________________

_______________________________________________________________________

26. What does the sign in Figure 45 tell you? ___________________________

_______________________________________________________________________

_______________________________________________________________________

Figure 46

Figure 47

Figure 48

Figure 49

27. What are the shape and color of regulatory signs? ______________________

_______________________________________________________________________

28. What does a symbol covered by a red circle and slash mean?

_______________________________________________________________________

29. What does Figure 46 tell you? ________________________________________

_______________________________________________________________________

30. What does Figure 47 tell you? ________________________________________

_______________________________________________________________________

31. What does Figure 48 tell you? ________________________________________

_______________________________________________________________________

32. What does Figure 49 tell you? ________________________________________

_______________________________________________________________________

Figure 50

Figure 51

33. What is the shape and color of warning signs (except for the school and school crossing signs)?

_______________________________________________________________________

34. What does Figure 50 warn you? _______________________________________

_______________________________________________________________________

35. What does Figure 51 warn you? _______________________________________

_______________________________________________________________________

Figure 52

Figure 53

Figure 54

Figure 55



36. What does Figure 52 warn you? _______________________________

_______________________________________________________________

37. What does Figure 53 warn you? _______________________________

_______________________________________________________________

38. What does Figure 54 warn you? _______________________________

_______________________________________________________________

39. What does Figure 55 warn you? _______________________________

_______________________________________________________________

Figure 56

Figure 57

40. What are guide signs? _______________________________________

_______________________________________________________________

41. What is the sign in Figure 56 called? _________________________

What does it tell you? _________________________________________

_______________________________________________________________

42. What does the sign in Figure 57 tell you? _____________________

_______________________________________________________________

Figure 58

Figure 59

43. What does the sign in Figure 58 tell you? _______________________________________

_______________________________________________________________________________

44. What does the sign in Figure 59 tell you? _______________________________________

_______________________________________________________________________________

## Traffic signals

45. What does a steady red light or a steady red arrow mean?

_______________________________________________________________________________

46. What does a steady yellow light alone or a steady yellow arrow mean?

_______________________________________________________________________________

47. What does a green light alone mean? _______________________________________

_______________________________________________________________________________

48. What does a green arrow in a traffic signal mean? _______________________________

_______________________________________________________________________________

49. What does a flashing red light tell you? _______________________________________

_______________________________________________________________________________

50. What does a flashing yellow light tell you? _____________________________________

_______________________________________________________________________________

51. What must you obey over all signals and signs? _____________________

______________________________________________________

## Pavement markings

52. What does a single, solid white line tell you? _____________________

______________________________________________________

______________________________________________________

53. When may you cross a single, solid white line? _____________________

______________________________________________________

______________________________________________________

54. What do a single, solid yellow line and a broken, yellow line tell?

______________________________________________________

______________________________________________________

55. What does a double, solid, yellow line tell you? _____________________

______________________________________________________

______________________________________________________

56. What lines show change in pavement width or number of lanes?

______________________________________________________

## Parking

57. What does a NO STOPPING sign mean? _____________________

______________________________________________________

58. What does a NO STANDING sign mean? _____________________

______________________________________________________

59. What does a NO PARKING sign mean? _____________________

______________________________________________________

60. When can there be no stopping, no standing, or no parking?

    a. ____________________________________________

    b. ____________________________________________

    c. ____________________________________________

    d. ____________________________________________

    e. ____________________________________________

61. You must not stand or park within how many feet of a crosswalk at an intersection?

_________________________________________________

62. Where can there be no standing or parking?

    a. ____________________________________________

    b. ____________________________________________

63. Where can there be no parking?

    a. ____________________________________________

    b. ____________________________________________

64. Within how many inches of the curb must you park? _________________________

65. How should you leave your car parked between two cars?

_________________________________________________

# Backing up

66. What should you do before backing up? _________________________

_________________________________________________

67. If there is any chance a child is behind your car, what should you do before backing up?

_________________________________________________

68. Can you back up into an open highway or expressway?

_________________________________________________

# Pedestrians

69. If there are no sidewalks, which side of the road should you walk on? ______________

______________

70. When does a blind person have the right-of-way crossing a street?

______________

______________

# Defensive driving

71. What does the defensive driver anticipate? ______________

______________

72. What does the defensive driver expect the other driver to do?

______________

# Speed and following distances

73. Unless otherwise posted, what is the maximum speed limit in your state? ______________

74. What does a minimum speed mean? ______________

______________

75. Why are minimum speeds sometimes used? ______________

______________

76. At least how far behind the vehicle ahead should a driver stay?

______________

77. At 40 miles per hour, how many car lengths behind the car ahead should you stay?

______________

# Vehicle condition

78. At least how much tread must a tire have? ______________

79. At 20 miles per hour, brakes must stop a car within how many feet? ______________

80. What is a warning signal that brakes need adjusting? _______________

_______________________________________________________________________

# Driver's physical condition

81. What should you do if you get drowsy while driving?

_______________________________________________________________________

_______________________________________________________________________

82. How does the use of alcohol adversely affect your driving?

_______________________________________________________________________

_______________________________________________________________________

_______________________________________________________________________

83. How much is safe to drink? _______________________________________

_______________________________________________________________________

84. What are some things you can do to control the effects of drinking?

    a. _________________________________________________________________

    b. _________________________________________________________________

    c. _________________________________________________________________

85. What could happen to you if you are convicted of driving while intoxicated (or, driving while under the influence of alcohol)?

    a. _________________________________________________________________

    b. _________________________________________________________________

    c. _________________________________________________________________

    d. _________________________________________________________________

    e. _________________________________________________________________

86. What drugs besides alcohol can make you an unsafe driver?

_______________________________________________________________________

_______________________________________________________________________

# Safety precautions

87. What are some safety precautions all drivers should take?

   a. _______________________________________

   b. _______________________________________

   c. _______________________________________

   d. _______________________________________

88. How should young children travel in a vehicle? _______________

_______________________________________

# Expressway driving

89. How does expressway driving differ from ordinary driving?

_______________________________________

_______________________________________

90. What is the purpose of the acceleration lane? _______________

_______________________________________

91. What is the purpose of the deceleration lane? _______________

_______________________________________

92. Give four expressway driving tips.

   a. _______________________________________

   b. _______________________________________

   c. _______________________________________

   d. _______________________________________

93. What is the first thing you should do if your vehicle breaks down on an expressway?

_______________________________________

# Special driving conditions

94. Why is night driving so dangerous? _______________________________________

_________________________________________________________________________

95. What lights must you use during hours of darkness?

_________________________________________________________________________

96. You must drop your headlights to low beam when you are within how many feet of an approaching vehicle?

_________________________________________________________________________

97. You must drop your headlights to low beam when you are within how many feet of a vehicle that you are following?

_________________________________________________________________________

98. If you start to skid on a slippery surface, should you use your brakes? _______________

99. What should you do if you start to skid on a slippery surface?

_________________________________________________________________________

100. How should you set your headlights in fog? _______________________________

_________________________________________________________________________

# Handling driving emergencies

101. What is the one basic rule that applies in all driving situations and especially in emergency situations?

_________________________________________________________________________

102. What should you do in case of a blowout? _______________________________

_________________________________________________________________________

103. What should you do if your brakes fail? _________________________________

_________________________________________________________________________

104. What should you do if your wheels run off the pavement?

_________________________________________________________________________

105. What should you do if a car approaches you in your lane?

_________________________________________________


# If you are involved in an accident

106. If involved in an accident with another driver, what information should you exchange
with the other driver?

    a. _________________________________________________

    b. _________________________________________________

    c. _________________________________________________

    d. _________________________________________________

107. What accidents must be reported in writing to the state?

    a. _________________________________________________

    b. _________________________________________________

108. How soon after an accident must you make the written report to the state?

_________________________________________________

# Sample Questions

These questions are much like the questions on the written driver's test you will take.

When doing the questions, write your answers on a separate sheet of paper. That way, you will be able to use the questions over again as many times as needed.

The questions cover subjects in the same order as the **Review of Driver's Manual**. The first column below lists the sample questions by section. The second column tells you where you can find the answers to those questions. This makes it easy to look back and go over the sections where you made mistakes.

| Sample questions | | Section of Review of Driver's Manual |
|---|---|---|
| 1 – 4 | .......... | Drive to the right |
| 5 – 13 | .......... | Passing other vehicles |
| 14 – 19 | .......... | Right-of-way |
| 20 – 28 | .......... | Turning |
| 29 – 47 | .......... | Traffic signs |
| 48 – 58 | .......... | Traffic signals |
| 59 – 64 | .......... | Pavement markings |
| 65 – 73 | .......... | Parking |
| 74 – 76 | .......... | Backing up |
| 77 – 78 | .......... | Pedestrians |
| 79 – 80 | .......... | Defensive driving |
| 81 – 86 | .......... | Speed and following distances |
| 87 – 89 | .......... | Vehicle condition |
| 90 – 95 | .......... | Driver's physical condition |
| 96 – 97 | .......... | Safety precautions |
| 98 – 101 | .......... | Expressway driving |
| 102 – 109 | .......... | Special driving conditions |
| 110 – 114 | .......... | Handling driving emergencies |
| 115 – 117 | .......... | If you are involved in an accident |

1. When may you drive to the left?

   a. When you are approaching a curve.
   b. When there is a double solid line.
   c. When you are 75 feet from a railroad crossing.
   d. When on a highway of more than two lanes where the right lane is for slow-moving traffic.

2. When may you not enter the opposing lane?

   a. When passing a vehicle.
   b. When approaching the crest of a hill.
   c. When making a left turn.
   d. When directed by a police officer.

3. When may you not drive to the left?

   a. When on a highway of more than two lanes.
   b. When on a one-way street.
   c. When passing a vehicle.
   d. When pavement markings prohibit it.

4. You may not enter the opposing lane of traffic when you are within how many feet of a railroad crossing?

   a. 100
   b. 200
   c. 300
   d. 400

5. In order to pass another vehicle safely, what is the minimum number of feet there should be between you and an oncoming car after you complete the pass?

   a. 50
   b. 100
   c. 200
   d. 300

6. After passing a car, do not swing back until:

   a. you see the car's front bumper in your side view mirror.
   b. you see the car when you turn your head.
   c. you see the side of the car on your right.
   d. you have traveled at least 500 feet.

7. When may you pass a car that is stopped for a pedestrian at a crosswalk?

   a. When the pedestrian sees you approaching.
   b. Never.
   c. When the pedestrian is just starting to cross.
   d. When you drive very slowly and carefully.

8. You are about to pass a car. You should:

   a. pull to the right.
   b. slow down.
   c. signal that you are going to pass.
   d. look in the rear view mirror and wait until you see the bumper of the car behind you.

9. You may pass a vehicle on the right when the vehicle:

   a. is making a left turn.
   b. is making a right turn.
   c. is going very slowly.
   d. is passing another car.

10. You may pass a vehicle on the right:

   a. when you signal that you are going to pass.
   b. when you sound your horn first.
   c. when the vehicle you are passing has stopped for a pedestrian at a crosswalk.
   d. when on a road with two or more lanes in each direction.

11. When may you pass a stopped school bus?

   a. Never.
   b. When waved on by a police officer.
   c. When the children getting off do not cross the street.
   d. When you use extreme caution.

12. When you are passed by another vehicle, you should:

   a. pull to your left and slow down slightly.
   b. stay to your right, but don't go off the pavement, and slow down slightly.
   c. stay to your right and pull off the pavement slightly and slow down.
   d. stay to your right and speed up slightly.

13. You should never do this when you are being passed:

   a. slow down.
   b. stay to the right.
   c. pull to the left.
   d. drive defensively.

14. Generally, at an intersection which has no traffic control device:

   a. the car on your right has the right-of-way.
   b. you have the right-of-way over a car on your right.
   c. all cars at the intersection have the right-of-way.
   d. the vehicle entering the intersection has the right-of-way over a vehicle already in the
      intersection.

15. You are approaching an intersection with a traffic control device. The light is green for you. Which of these has the right-of-way?

   a. The car on your right.
   b. You have the right-of-way.
   c. The car closest to the intersection.
   d. The car on your left.

16. Which of these has the right-of-way over all the others?

   a. The car already in the intersection.
   b. The car going straight ahead.
   c. The vehicle already in a traffic circle.
   d. An emergency vehicle.

17. Which of these has the right-of-way over the others?

   a. A car going straight ahead.
   b. A car turning right.
   c. A car entering a main road from a private road.
   d. A pedestrian in a crosswalk.

18. A car going straight ahead has the right-of-way over:

   a. a car turning left.
   b. a fire engine.
   c. a pedestrian in a crosswalk.
   d. an ambulance.

19. When should you insist on your having the right-of-way?

   a. When you are in a traffic circle.
   b. Never, if it will create a dangerous situation.
   c. When you are the car on the right.
   d. When you are going straight ahead.

20. How many feet before making a turn must you signal your intention of doing so?

   a. 75
   b. 100
   c. 200
   d. 250

21. If approaching traffic prevents your making a left turn immediately, you should:

   a. pull in front of an oncoming car so he will have to stop and let you make the turn.
   b. keep going straight ahead and turn at the next intersection.
   c. pull over to the right side of the road and wait there for traffic to clear.
   d. move into the center of the intersection in your lane and wait there for the traffic to clear.

22. U-turns are prohibited:

    a. on all two lane roads.
    b. only where a NO U-TURN sign is posted.
    c. near the crest of a hill.
    d. by a shopping mall.

23. In making a right turn:

    a. approach the turn as close as possible to the right curb.
    b. approach the turn as close as possible to the center line.
    c. approach the turn as close as possible to the left curb.
    d. approach the turn from the middle of the intersection.

24. In making a left turn from a one-way road onto another one-way road:

    a. approach the turn as close as possible to the left curb.
    b. approach the turn as close as possible to the center line.
    c. approach the turn as close as possible to the right curb.
    d. approach the turn from the middle of the intersection.

25. In making a left turn from a two-way road onto a one-way road:

    a. approach the turn from the middle of the intersection.
    b. approach the turn as close as possible to the center line.
    c. approach the turn as close as possible to the left curb.
    d. approach the turn as close as possible to the right curb.

26. In making a left turn from a two-way road onto a two-way road:

    a. approach the turn from the left lane.
    b. drive up to the turn as far to the right as possible.
    c. approach the turn from the right lane.
    d. approach the turn as close as possible to the center line.

27. In making a left turn from a one-way road onto a two-way road:

    a. approach the turn in the right lane.
    b. approach the turn in the left lane.
    c. turn before you reach the middle of the intersection.
    d. turn as close to the left curb as you can.

28. In making a left turn from a two-way road onto a four-lane highway:

    a. turn into the passing lane.
    b. turn into the right lane.
    c. approach the turn from as far right as possible.
    d. make the turn before you reach the middle of the intersection.

1      2      3      4      5

29. What does the sign in Figure 1 mean?

    a. Stop only for traffic on an intersecting road.
    b. Come to a full stop, then go when it is safe to do so.
    c. Slow down and prepare to stop only if cars are approaching.
    d. Stop and wait for the green light to follow.

30. What does the sign in Figure 2 mean?

    a. There is no right turn.
    b. Slow down and stop before turning if cars are approaching.
    c. Come to a full stop, then proceed when it's safe to do so.
    d. Slow down and proceed to turn when it is safe to do so.

31. The sign in Figure 3 does not tell us to:

    a. do everything you would at a stop sign.
    b. give up the right-of-way.
    c. stop if necessary.
    d. slow down.

32. The sign in Figure 4 means:

    a. come to a full stop at the railroad crossing.
    b. do not cross the railroad tracks.
    c. cross the railroad tracks as quickly as possible before a train comes.
    d. be prepared to slow down and possibly stop at the railroad crossing.

33. What does the sign in Figure 5 mean?

    a. Come to a full stop at the school crossing.
    b. It warns that you are approaching a school crossing.
    c. Slow down and be prepared to pass any school buses that might be stopped at the school crossing.
    d. Do not exceed 10 mph in the school crossing zone.

34. Where do you stop if an intersection has a stop sign but no stop line?

    a. In the crosswalk.
    b. Before the crosswalk.
    c. Just past the crosswalk.
    d. In the intersection, past the crosswalk.

35. Where do you stop if an intersection has a stop sign but no stop line and no crosswalk?

   a. Stop at least 50 feet before the intersection.
   b. Stop so that all the vehicle is in the intersection.
   c. Stop so that the front wheels cross into the intersection.
   d. Stop near the intersection where you can see the traffic.

36. What does a yield sign mean?

   a. Maintain the same speed but get ready to stop and give up the right-of-way.
   b. Maintain the same speed and continue through the intersection because you have the right-of-way.
   c. Slow down, get ready to stop, and give up the right-of-way.
   d. Stop completely and wait for the green arrow.

37. A yield sign is the same as a stop sign except:

   a. a yield sign is not found at an intersection.
   b. you do not have to come to a full stop unless necessary.
   c. you do not have to yield the right-of-way to vehicles.
   d. you do not have to yield the right-of-way to pedestrians.

38. Regulatory signs:

   a. warn you of something.
   b. give route numbers.
   c. give distances.
   d. tell you the rules about what you can do.

39. What shape are regulatory signs?

   a. Diamond-shaped.
   b. Triangular.
   c. Rectangular.
   d. Five-sided.

40. Which of these would be a regulatory sign?

   a. NARROW BRIDGE
   b. SPEED LIMIT 55
   c. ROAD CURVES
   d. FALLEN ROCK ZONE

41. Which of these would not be a regulatory sign?

   a. NO U TURN
   b. DO NOT PASS
   c. STEEP HILL
   d. NO RIGHT TURN

42. What is the shape of warning signs (except for the school and school crossing signs)?

   a. Rectangular.
   b. Diamond-shaped.
   c. Round.
   d. Five-sided.

43. What do warning signs tell us?

   a. They tell us how or what to do.
   b. They warn us of some physical hazard.
   c. They tell us where not to park.
   d. They tell us distances to towns and cities.

44. Which of these would be a warning sign?

   a. YIELD
   b. NO STOPPING
   c. NO TURN ON RED
   d. FALLEN ROCK ZONE

45. Which of these would not be a warning sign?

   a. SOFT SHOULDER
   b. DEAD END
   c. NO TURNS
   d. NO OUTLET

46. What do destination signs look like?

   a. They are white, rectangular signs with green lettering.
   b. They are green, rectangular signs with white lettering.
   c. They are white, square signs with green lettering.
   d. They are green, square signs with white lettering.

47. Destination signs tell us:

   a. distances to towns and cities.
   b. the numbers of state routes.
   c. information about food and gas.
   d. the number of the next interstate.

48. A steady red light or steady red arrow means:

   a. stop and wait for the green light or arrow.
   b. come to a full stop and then proceed with caution.
   c. slow down and get ready to stop if necessary.
   d. do not enter.

49. A steady yellow light or steady yellow arrow means:

a. proceed with caution.
b. the same as a yield sign.
c. the same as a stop sign.
d. the red light will follow.

50. What light follows a steady yellow light?

a. Steady red.
b. Green.
c. Flashing red.
d. Flashing yellow.

51. What should you do when you approach an intersection and the traffic light changes from green to yellow?

a. Stop immediately.
b. Get ready to stop before the intersection because the red light will come on.
c. Speed up so you will get through the intersection before the red light comes on.
d. Stop and then proceed with caution.

52. A green arrow indicates:

a. that the road becomes one-way so all traffic must turn in the direction of the arrow.
b. that you must come to a full stop and then move in the direction of the arrow.
c. that you may move but only in the direction of the arrow.
d. the same as a green light.

53. A flashing red light has essentially the same meaning as:

a. a stop sign.
b. a yield sign.
c. a steady red light.
d. a steady yellow light.

54. A flashing red light means:

a. slow down and be ready to stop if necessary.
b. come to a full stop and wait for the green light.
c. come to a complete stop and proceed after yielding the right-of-way.
d. maintain the same speed but get ready to slow down if necessary.

55. What should you do when you approach an intersection with a flashing yellow light?

a. Slow down and give up the right-of-way.
b. Come to a complete stop and proceed after yielding the right-of-way.
c. Be ready to stop because the red light will follow.
d. Proceed with caution.

56. Which of the following must you obey over the other three?

    a. A stop sign.
    b. A flashing red light.
    c. A traffic officer.
    d. A steady red light.

57. What should you do if you are approaching an intersection where a traffic signal is red and a policeman motions you to go through?

    a. Wait for the green light.
    b. Go through the red light.
    c. Stop and tell the policeman he is telling you to break the law.
    d. Go through the red light but report the incident to police headquarters.

58. What does a flashing yellow light mean?

    a. Merging traffic.
    b. Pedestrian crossing.
    c. Proceed with caution.
    d. Come to a full stop.

59. When can you cross a single, broken, white or yellow line?

    a. Never.
    b. Only to make a left turn into or out of a driveway or alley.
    c. Only to pass another vehicle.
    d. When crossing will not interfere with traffic.

60. What does a single, solid, white line mean?

    a. It defines lanes. It shows you where the lanes are.
    b. It is a warning line that you should keep within the lane, but it may be crossed when traffic conditions are favorable.
    c. It means you may not cross it.
    d. You may cross it only when directed by a police officer.

61. What does a double, solid, yellow line mean?

    a. You may cross it if traffic permits.
    b. Do not cross in either direction except to make a left turn into or out of a driveway or alley.
    c. You are approaching a stop sign.
    d. The highway gets narrower.

62. What should you do when a broken, yellow line is on your side of a solid, yellow line?

    a. You may cross it if traffic permits.
    b. Do not cross it under any conditions.
    c. You may cross it only at an intersection.
    d. You may cross it only on expressways.

63. What should you do when a solid, yellow line is on your side of a broken, yellow line?

   a. Do not cross it except to make a left turn into or out of a driveway or alley.
   b. You may cross it if traffic permits.
   c. You may cross it only at an intersection.
   d. You may cross it only on expressways.

64. What does it mean when the solid line at the edge of the road moves inward diagonally?

   a. The highway gets wider.
   b. The highway gets narrower.
   c. You are approaching a bridge.
   d. You are coming to the end of an expressway.

65. What does a NO STOPPING sign mean?

   a. You may not stop for any purpose whatsoever.
   b. You may stop only to load or unload merchandise.
   c. You may not stop except when directed by a police officer.
   d. You may stop only to receive or discharge passengers.

66. What does a NO STANDING sign mean?

   a. You may stop only to receive or discharge passengers.
   b. You may stop only to load or unload merchandise.
   c. You may not stop for any purpose.
   d. You may stop only to load or unload merchandise or passengers.

67. When may you stop a vehicle in a NO PARKING area?

   a. Never.
   b. Only to load or unload merchandise or passengers.
   c. Only on orders of a police officer.
   d. Only when you stop in front of your house.

68. Where is stopping always forbidden?

   a. On a highway bridge.
   b. In front of a fire hydrant.
   c. Within 50 feet of a railroad crossing.
   d. In front of a driveway.

69. Where is stopping always forbidden?

   a. Within 30 feet of a railroad crossing.
   b. In front of a driveway.
   c. Within 15 feet of a fire hydrant.
   d. On a crosswalk.

70. What is the closest distance you may park to a fire hydrant?

    a.  5 feet.
    b. 10 feet.
    c. 12 feet.
    d. 15 feet.

71. Where is it all right to stop temporarily, but not to park?

    a. On a sidewalk.
    b. Within an intersection.
    c. In front of a driveway.
    d. On railroad tracks.

72. Within how many inches of the curb must you park?

    a.  6
    b. 10
    c. 12
    d. 18

73. What should you do after you back your car into a parking space between two cars?

    a. Leave the car in neutral with the parking brake off.
    b. Back up and leave the car almost touching the car behind.
    c. Move forward as far as possible.
    d. Leave enough space between the two cars.

74. What should you do before backing up?

    a. Look into the sideview mirror.
    b. Check the rearview mirror.
    c. Check your mirrors and then turn your head and look back.
    d. Sound your horn.

75. If there is any chance a child may be behind your car, what should you do before you back up?

    a. Sound your horn.
    b. Get out and walk to the back of the car.
    c. Pull ahead a few feet before you back up.
    d. Check the mirrors two or three times.

76. When may you back up on the pavement of an open highway or expressway?

    a. Never.
    b. When you do not see any traffic.
    c. Only after you have signaled your intention of backing up.
    d. When you back up and pull ahead very quickly.

77. When there are no sidewalks, which side of the road should a pedestrian walk on?

    a. On the same side of the road as the traffic is moving.
    b. On the right side of the road.
    c. On the side of the road facing oncoming traffic.
    d. On the side of the road with lighter traffic.

78. When does a blind person have the right-of-way?

    a. When he is wearing dark glasses.
    b. When he is being helped by another person.
    c. When he is using a white cane or is being led by a seeing-eye dog.
    d. When he is wearing light-colored clothing and carrying a light.

79. What does defensive driving mean?

    a. Always insist on the right-of-way.
    b. Always go slower than the maximum speed.
    c. Always let the other cars go first.
    d. Anticipate errors by others and be ready to react to mistakes.

80. The defensive driver follows this rule:

    a. give all your attention to your own driving.
    b. expect the other driver to do the wrong thing.
    c. do not drive in heavy traffic.
    d. always insist on the right-of-way.

81. Unless otherwise posted, the maximum speed is:

    a. 50 mph.
    b. 55 mph.
    c. 60 mph.
    d. 65 mph.

82. Why are minimum speed limits sometimes posted?

    a. To keep vehicles from speeding.
    b. To increase the safety of pedestrians.
    c. To prevent rear-end collisions.
    d. To warn you of slow-moving vehicles.

83. If a minimum speed is posted, you should:

    a. go slower than the minimum speed.
    b. not go slower than the minimum speed.
    c. not go over or under the speed posted.
    d. go at least 25 miles over the minimum speed.

84. When selecting a speed to travel at, you should consider:

    a. the maximum and minimum speed limits.
    b. the conditions of the road, your vehicle, and yourself.
    c. the flow of traffic.
    d. all of the above.

85. At 50 miles per hour, how many car lengths should you allow between your car and the one ahead?

    a. At least 5.
    b. At least 3.
    c. At least 6.
    d. At least 2.

86. At 40 miles per hour, how many car lengths should you allow between your car and the one ahead?

    a. At least 4.
    b. At least 3.
    c. At least 5.
    d. At least 6.

87. If, when you apply your brakes, the vehicle pulls to one side, the cause is probably:

    a. worn steering mechanism.
    b. a bad tire.
    c. faulty brakes.
    d. a worn muffler.

88. Within how many feet must the foot brakes stop a car going 20 miles per hour?

    a. 25 feet.
    b. 30 feet.
    c. 40 feet.
    d. 50 feet.

89. All tires must have at least how much tread?

    a. 3/16 of an inch.
    b. 2/16 of an inch.
    c. 1/32 of an inch.
    d. 2/32 of an inch.

90. If you feel yourself getting drowsy while driving, it is a good idea to:

    a. speed up so you will get to your destination sooner.
    b. cut in and out of traffic so you will be more active and less bored.
    c. follow the car ahead and stay close to it.
    d. open the window, and stop for a rest and a walk.

91. What effect does the drinking of alcohol have on your ability to drive?

    a. It slows reflexes and impairs vision and judgment.
    b. It impairs vision but speeds up reflexes.
    c. It slows reflexes but improves vision and judgment.
    d. It relaxes the driver and improves his driving skills.

92. How much is safe to drink when driving:

    a. one drink per hour.
    b. depends on what you're drinking.
    c. is the same for everyone.
    d. is not the same for everyone.

93. Something you can do to control the effects of drinking is:

    a. drink quickly so your body can get rid of the alcohol faster.
    b. drink only beer.
    c. eat some food.
    d. drink only wine.

94. The penalty for drunk driving is:

    a. a fine.
    b. a jail sentence.
    c. loss of license.
    d. possibly all of the above.

95. The following may affect your ability to drive safely:

    a. alcohol.
    b. alcohol and illegal drugs.
    c. prescription drugs and drug-store medicines.
    d. alcohol, prescription drugs, drug-store medicines, and illegal drugs.

96. A precaution that all drivers should take every time they drive is to:

    a. have the oil checked.
    b. have the brakes checked.
    c. wear their seatbelt.
    d. listen to the traffic report.

97. Young children when in a vehicle should:

    a. ride in their mother's arms.
    b. ride in the front seat between their parents or two adults.
    c. ride in the back seat.
    d. ride in an approved child restraint seat.

98. What is the principal difference between expressway driving and ordinary driving?

   a. Trucks cannot use expressways.
   b. Traffic is heavier on expressways.
   c. Expressway driving is more dangerous.
   d. The speed limit is higher on expressways.

99. What is the purpose of an expressway acceleration lane?

   a. It allows drivers to test their cars before entering the expressway.
   b. It allows drivers to speed up to cruising speed before merging with the traffic.
   c. It gives drivers a chance to pass slow-moving vehicles.
   d. It allows drivers to get used to the higher speeds.

100. Which of these is an expressway driving tip?

   a. Keep windows closed so a bee cannot fly in.
   b. Wear good sunglasses at night to cut down the glare of headlights.
   c. Keep going at a steady speed and do not stop and rest.
   d. Stop and rest when drowsy.

101. What is the first thing you should do if your car breaks down on an expressway?

   a. Get off the pavement.
   b. Use color-coded balloons.
   c. Put a cloth on a door handle or antenna.
   d. Turn on parking lights.

102. During hours of darkness, you must always use:

   a. headlights and parking lights.
   b. headlights, except in fog, use the parking lights.
   c. headlights.
   d. headlights on high beam except in fog.

103. Why is night driving so dangerous?

   a. There is more traffic at night.
   b. The amount we see is greatly reduced.
   c. Many people drink alcohol at night.
   d. There is less traffic so people speed.

104. Within how many feet of an approaching vehicle must you drop your headlights to low beam?

   a. 200 feet.
   b. 350 feet.
   c. 400 feet.
   d. 500 feet.

105. Within how many feet of a vehicle that you are following must you drop your headlights to low beam?

a. 500 feet.
b. 400 feet.
c. 300 feet.
d. 200 feet.

106. What should you do if your vehicle starts to skid on a slippery surface?

a. Steer gently into the skid without using your brakes.
b. Steer gently into the skid and brake hard.
c. Steer gently away from the side without braking.
d. Use the brakes, but go very easy on the pedal.

107. If your vehicle starts to skid on a slippery surface, you should:

a. steer away from the skid.
b. decelerate abruptly.
c. steer into the skid.
d. use your brakes.

108. What does the sign SNOW EMERGENCY STREET mean?

a. In a snowstorm, only emergency vehicles may use the street.
b. Snow tires or chains must be used.
c. Do not use this street because it is being plowed.
d. You must have chains to use this street.

109. How should you drive in heavy fog?

a. Use your headlights on low beam.
b. Use your headlights on high beam.
c. Use only parking lights so there will be no reflection to blind you.
d. Stay to the middle of the road because the side of the road is difficult to see.

110. What is the one basic rule that applies in all emergency situations?

a. Your first reaction is the best.
b. Use your brakes immediately.
c. Act first because you do not have time to think.
d. Think before you act.

111. What should you do if you have a tire blowout?

a. Hold tightly to the steering wheel and brake.
b. Hold tightly to the steering wheel, and ease up on the gas. Do not brake.
c. Hold tightly to the steering wheel and keep going at the same speed.
d. Hold tightly to the steering wheel and quickly swerve off the road.

112. What should you do if your wheels go off the pavement onto the shoulder of the road?

   a. Stay on the shoulder and ease up on the gas.
   b. Stay on the shoulder and quickly apply the brakes.
   c. Swerve completely off the pavement.
   d. Quickly swerve back on the pavement.

113. What is the one thing you should not do if your wheels go off the pavement onto the shoulder of the road?

   a. Stay on the shoulder.
   b. Ease up on the gas.
   c. Swerve back on the pavement.
   d. Think before you act.

114. What is the one thing you should not do if a car approaches you in your lane?

   a. Pull to the right.
   b. Slow down and honk your horn.
   c. Flash your lights.
   d. Turn into his lane.

115. What are all the circumstances under which you must make a written report of an accident to the state?

   a. Death.
   b. Death or personal injury.
   c. Death or personal injury or property damage over $100.
   d. Death or personal injury or property damage over $400.

116. If you are involved in an accident and there is not death or personal injury, what amount of property damage must be reported to the state in writing?

   a. Over $100.
   b. Over $400.
   c. Over $ 50.
   d. Over $300.

117. If you are involved in an accident which must be reported, how soon must you make the report to the state?

   a. Within 30 days.
   b. Within 5 days.
   c. Within 15 days.
   d. Within 10 days.

# Sample Tests

These tests are made up of different combinations of questions from the Sample Questions on pages 36-52.

There are 20 different tests. Each test has three columns:

Column 1 — numbers the questions in each test.

Column 2 — gives the number of the sample questions you should use.

For example, for question 1 in Test 1, you should use sample question 4 on page 36.

Column 3 — is where you write your answers.

When you finish a test, you can correct it yourself. Answer keys are on page 64. But don't cheat and look at an answer before you finish taking the test. Remember, you want to see how you would do if this were the actual written test for your driver's license.

Each test has 20 questions. So each question is worth 5 points. To find out your score, take the number of questions you have answered correctly and multiply it by 5. The answer will be your score. A score of 75 or more is passing.

# Directions

Remember, Column 2 tells you which questions from the Sample Questions on pages 36-52 to answer for the test. Write your answers in Column 3.

Each question is worth 5 points. A score of 75 is PASSING. To find your score, take the number of questions you answered correctly and multiply it by 5.

### Test 1

| | | |
|---|---|---|
| 1 | 4 | |
| 2 | 7 | |
| 3 | 19 | |
| 4 | 26 | |
| 5 | 36 | |
| 6 | 44 | |
| 7 | 57 | |
| 8 | 59 | |
| 9 | 65 | |
| 10 | 75 | |
| 11 | 77 | |
| 12 | 80 | |
| 13 | 84 | |
| 14 | 88 | |
| 15 | 90 | |
| 16 | 97 | |
| 17 | 99 | |
| 18 | 105 | |
| 19 | 111 | |
| 20 | 117 | |

No. Correct ☐  
×5 ☐  
SCORE ☐

### Test 2

| | | |
|---|---|---|
| 1 | 2 | |
| 2 | 9 | |
| 3 | 15 | |
| 4 | 28 | |
| 5 | 30 | |
| 6 | 42 | |
| 7 | 48 | |
| 8 | 61 | |
| 9 | 67 | |
| 10 | 76 | |
| 11 | 77 | |
| 12 | 80 | |
| 13 | 86 | |
| 14 | 89 | |
| 15 | 92 | |
| 16 | 97 | |
| 17 | 100 | |
| 18 | 107 | |
| 19 | 114 | |
| 20 | 116 | |

No. Correct ☐  
×5 ☐  
SCORE ☐

### Test 3

| | | |
|---|---|---|
| 1 | 1 | |
| 2 | 12 | |
| 3 | 18 | |
| 4 | 22 | |
| 5 | 33 | |
| 6 | 39 | |
| 7 | 51 | |
| 8 | 64 | |
| 9 | 70 | |
| 10 | 76 | |
| 11 | 78 | |
| 12 | 79 | |
| 13 | 83 | |
| 14 | 89 | |
| 15 | 95 | |
| 16 | 96 | |
| 17 | 100 | |
| 18 | 108 | |
| 19 | 112 | |
| 20 | 116 | |

No. Correct ☐  
×5 ☐  
SCORE ☐

### Test 4

| | | |
|---|---|---|
| 1 | 3 | |
| 2 | 5 | |
| 3 | 14 | |
| 4 | 24 | |
| 5 | 35 | |
| 6 | 37 | |
| 7 | 53 | |
| 8 | 60 | |
| 9 | 72 | |
| 10 | 75 | |
| 11 | 78 | |
| 12 | 80 | |
| 13 | 85 | |
| 14 | 88 | |
| 15 | 91 | |
| 16 | 96 | |
| 17 | 101 | |
| 18 | 106 | |
| 19 | 114 | |
| 20 | 115 | |

No. Correct ☐  
×5 ☐  
SCORE ☐

# Directions

Remember, Column 2 tells you which questions from the Sample Questions on pages 36-52 to answer for the test. Write your answers in Column 3.

Each question is worth 5 points. A score of 75 is PASSING. To find your score, take the number of questions you answered correctly and multiply it by 5.

### Test 5

| | | |
|---|---|---|
| 1 | 1 | |
| 2 | 7 | |
| 3 | 16 | |
| 4 | 26 | |
| 5 | 29 | |
| 6 | 39 | |
| 7 | 55 | |
| 8 | 62 | |
| 9 | 65 | |
| 10 | 75 | |
| 11 | 78 | |
| 12 | 79 | |
| 13 | 81 | |
| 14 | 89 | |
| 15 | 92 | |
| 16 | 96 | |
| 17 | 98 | |
| 18 | 105 | |
| 19 | 113 | |
| 20 | 117 | |

**No. Correct**

×5

**SCORE**

### Test 6

| | | |
|---|---|---|
| 1 | 2 | |
| 2 | 12 | |
| 3 | 15 | |
| 4 | 22 | |
| 5 | 34 | |
| 6 | 44 | |
| 7 | 49 | |
| 8 | 61 | |
| 9 | 68 | |
| 10 | 76 | |
| 11 | 77 | |
| 12 | 80 | |
| 13 | 86 | |
| 14 | 87 | |
| 15 | 92 | |
| 16 | 97 | |
| 17 | 98 | |
| 18 | 107 | |
| 19 | 112 | |
| 20 | 117 | |

**No. Correct**

×5

**SCORE**

### Test 7

| | | |
|---|---|---|
| 1 | 3 | |
| 2 | 6 | |
| 3 | 18 | |
| 4 | 25 | |
| 5 | 35 | |
| 6 | 45 | |
| 7 | 56 | |
| 8 | 64 | |
| 9 | 73 | |
| 10 | 76 | |
| 11 | 78 | |
| 12 | 79 | |
| 13 | 83 | |
| 14 | 87 | |
| 15 | 95 | |
| 16 | 96 | |
| 17 | 98 | |
| 18 | 104 | |
| 19 | 110 | |
| 20 | 116 | |

**No. Correct**

×5

**SCORE**

### Test 8

| | | |
|---|---|---|
| 1 | 4 | |
| 2 | 11 | |
| 3 | 17 | |
| 4 | 21 | |
| 5 | 32 | |
| 6 | 40 | |
| 7 | 50 | |
| 8 | 63 | |
| 9 | 69 | |
| 10 | 75 | |
| 11 | 77 | |
| 12 | 80 | |
| 13 | 82 | |
| 14 | 87 | |
| 15 | 91 | |
| 16 | 97 | |
| 17 | 99 | |
| 18 | 109 | |
| 19 | 111 | |
| 20 | 116 | |

**No. Correct**

×5

**SCORE**

# Directions

Remember, Column 2 tells you which questions from the Sample Questions on pages 36-52 to answer for the test. Write your answers in Column 3.

Each question is worth 5 points. A score of 75 is PASSING. To find your score, take the number of questions you answered correctly and multiply it by 5.

| Test 9 | | | Test 10 | | | Test 11 | | | Test 12 | | |
|---|---|---|---|---|---|---|---|---|---|---|---|
| 1 | 1 | | 1 | 2 | | 1 | 3 | | 1 | 4 | |
| 2 | 11 | | 2 | 5 | | 2 | 10 | | 2 | 6 | |
| 3 | 14 | | 3 | 17 | | 3 | 16 | | 3 | 15 | |
| 4 | 21 | | 4 | 24 | | 4 | 20 | | 4 | 25 | |
| 5 | 33 | | 5 | 34 | | 5 | 31 | | 5 | 36 | |
| 6 | 43 | | 6 | 46 | | 6 | 41 | | 6 | 38 | |
| 7 | 48 | | 7 | 55 | | 7 | 49 | | 7 | 54 | |
| 8 | 60 | | 8 | 63 | | 8 | 62 | | 8 | 61 | |
| 9 | 71 | | 9 | 72 | | 9 | 68 | | 9 | 73 | |
| 10 | 76 | | 10 | 75 | | 10 | 74 | | 10 | 76 | |
| 11 | 78 | | 11 | 77 | | 11 | 78 | | 11 | 77 | |
| 12 | 80 | | 12 | 79 | | 12 | 79 | | 12 | 79 | |
| 13 | 85 | | 13 | 82 | | 13 | 81 | | 13 | 86 | |
| 14 | 87 | | 14 | 88 | | 14 | 87 | | 14 | 88 | |
| 15 | 93 | | 15 | 94 | | 15 | 93 | | 15 | 93 | |
| 16 | 96 | | 16 | 97 | | 16 | 96 | | 16 | 97 | |
| 17 | 100 | | 17 | 101 | | 17 | 101 | | 17 | 99 | |
| 18 | 104 | | 18 | 109 | | 18 | 108 | | 18 | 108 | |
| 19 | 113 | | 19 | 114 | | 19 | 110 | | 19 | 114 | |
| 20 | 117 | | 20 | 115 | | 20 | 117 | | 20 | 117 | |
| **No. Correct** | | | **No. Correct** | | | **No. Correct** | | | **No. Correct** | | |
| | | ×5 | | | ×5 | | | ×5 | | | ×5 |
| **SCORE** | | | **SCORE** | | | **SCORE** | | | **SCORE** | | |

# Directions

Remember, Column 2 tells you which questions from the Sample Questions on pages 36-52 to answer for the test. Write your answers in Column 3.

Each question is worth 5 points. A score of 75 is PASSING. To find your score, take the number of questions you answered correctly and multiply it by 5.

**Test 13**

| | | |
|---|---|---|
| 1 | 1 | |
| 2 | 6 | |
| 3 | 16 | |
| 4 | 23 | |
| 5 | 33 | |
| 6 | 47 | |
| 7 | 54 | |
| 8 | 62 | |
| 9 | 71 | |
| 10 | 74 | |
| 11 | 78 | |
| 12 | 79 | |
| 13 | 81 | |
| 14 | 89 | |
| 15 | 93 | |
| 16 | 96 | |
| 17 | 100 | |
| 18 | 102 | |
| 19 | 112 | |
| 20 | 117 | |

**No. Correct**
×5
**SCORE**

**Test 14**

| | | |
|---|---|---|
| 1 | 3 | |
| 2 | 13 | |
| 3 | 19 | |
| 4 | 23 | |
| 5 | 34 | |
| 6 | 38 | |
| 7 | 52 | |
| 8 | 59 | |
| 9 | 71 | |
| 10 | 74 | |
| 11 | 77 | |
| 12 | 80 | |
| 13 | 84 | |
| 14 | 87 | |
| 15 | 90 | |
| 16 | 97 | |
| 17 | 98 | |
| 18 | 107 | |
| 19 | 113 | |
| 20 | 116 | |

**No. Correct**
×5
**SCORE**

**Test 15**

| | | |
|---|---|---|
| 1 | 4 | |
| 2 | 9 | |
| 3 | 18 | |
| 4 | 28 | |
| 5 | 31 | |
| 6 | 47 | |
| 7 | 57 | |
| 8 | 64 | |
| 9 | 69 | |
| 10 | 74 | |
| 11 | 78 | |
| 12 | 79 | |
| 13 | 83 | |
| 14 | 87 | |
| 15 | 95 | |
| 16 | 96 | |
| 17 | 99 | |
| 18 | 102 | |
| 19 | 111 | |
| 20 | 115 | |

**No. Correct**
×5
**SCORE**

**Test 16**

| | | |
|---|---|---|
| 1 | 2 | |
| 2 | 5 | |
| 3 | 18 | |
| 4 | 24 | |
| 5 | 36 | |
| 6 | 46 | |
| 7 | 51 | |
| 8 | 63 | |
| 9 | 67 | |
| 10 | 74 | |
| 11 | 77 | |
| 12 | 80 | |
| 13 | 82 | |
| 14 | 89 | |
| 15 | 90 | |
| 16 | 97 | |
| 17 | 99 | |
| 18 | 103 | |
| 19 | 110 | |
| 20 | 116 | |

**No. Correct**
×5
**SCORE**

# Directions

Remember, Column 2 tells you which questions from the Sample Questions on pages 36-52 to answer for the test. Write your answers in Column 3.

Each question is worth 5 points. A score of 75 is PASSING. To find your score, take the number of questions you answered correctly and multiply it by 5.

**Test 17**

| | | |
|---|---|---|
| 1 | 2 | |
| 2 | 8 | |
| 3 | 17 | |
| 4 | 27 | |
| 5 | 30 | |
| 6 | 40 | |
| 7 | 56 | |
| 8 | 63 | |
| 9 | 66 | |
| 10 | 74 | |
| 11 | 77 | |
| 12 | 80 | |
| 13 | 82 | |
| 14 | 88 | |
| 15 | 94 | |
| 16 | 97 | |
| 17 | 100 | |
| 18 | 103 | |
| 19 | 112 | |
| 20 | 115 | |

No. Correct

×5

SCORE

**Test 18**

| | | |
|---|---|---|
| 1 | 1 | |
| 2 | 8 | |
| 3 | 14 | |
| 4 | 27 | |
| 5 | 29 | |
| 6 | 43 | |
| 7 | 58 | |
| 8 | 60 | |
| 9 | 66 | |
| 10 | 74 | |
| 11 | 78 | |
| 12 | 80 | |
| 13 | 85 | |
| 14 | 88 | |
| 15 | 91 | |
| 16 | 96 | |
| 17 | 98 | |
| 18 | 106 | |
| 19 | 113 | |
| 20 | 115 | |

No. Correct

×5

SCORE

**Test 19**

| | | |
|---|---|---|
| 1 | 3 | |
| 2 | 13 | |
| 3 | 16 | |
| 4 | 25 | |
| 5 | 30 | |
| 6 | 45 | |
| 7 | 50 | |
| 8 | 62 | |
| 9 | 73 | |
| 10 | 75 | |
| 11 | 78 | |
| 12 | 79 | |
| 13 | 81 | |
| 14 | 88 | |
| 15 | 94 | |
| 16 | 96 | |
| 17 | 101 | |
| 18 | 106 | |
| 19 | 111 | |
| 20 | 116 | |

No. Correct

×5

SCORE

**Test 20**

| | | |
|---|---|---|
| 1 | 4 | |
| 2 | 10 | |
| 3 | 19 | |
| 4 | 20 | |
| 5 | 32 | |
| 6 | 42 | |
| 7 | 58 | |
| 8 | 59 | |
| 9 | 70 | |
| 10 | 75 | |
| 11 | 77 | |
| 12 | 79 | |
| 13 | 84 | |
| 14 | 89 | |
| 15 | 94 | |
| 16 | 97 | |
| 17 | 101 | |
| 18 | 105 | |
| 19 | 110 | |
| 20 | 115 | |

No. Correct

×5

SCORE

# Answer Keys for Sample Tests

These answers are based on the New York state driver's manual. Answers left blank are different in different states. Look them up in your own state driver's manual.

| Test 1 | Test 2 | Test 3 | Test 4 | Test 5 |
|---|---|---|---|---|
| 1. a | 1. b | 1. d | 1. d | 1. d |
| 2. b | 2. a | 2. b | 2. c | 2. b |
| 3. b | 3. b | 3. a | 3. a | 3. d |
| 4. d | 4. a | 4. | 4. a | 4. d |
| 5. c | 5. a | 5. b | 5. d | 5. b |
| 6. d | 6. b | 6. c | 6. b | 6. c |
| 7. b | 7. a | 7. b | 7. a | 7. d |
| 8. d | 8. b | 8. b | 8. b | 8. a |
| 9. c | 9. b | 9. | 9. | 9. c |
| 10. b | 10. a | 10. a | 10. b | 10. b |
| 11. c | 11. c | 11. c | 11. c | 11. c |
| 12. b | 12. b | 12. d | 12. b | 12. d |
| 13. d | 13. a | 13. b | 13. a | 13. d |
| 14. | 14. d | 14. d | 14. | 14. d |
| 15. d | 15. d | 15. d | 15. a | 15. d |
| 16. d | 16. d | 16. c | 16. c | 16. c |
| 17. b | 17. d | 17. d | 17. a | 17. c |
| 18. | 18. c | 18. b | 18. a | 18. |
| 19. b | 19. d | 19. a | 19. d | 19. c |
| 20. | 20. | 20. | 20. | 20. |

| Test 6 | Test 7 | Test 8 | Test 9 | Test 10 |
|---|---|---|---|---|
| 1. b | 1. d | 1. a | 1. d | 1. b |
| 2. b | 2. d | 2. b | 2. b | 2. c |
| 3. b | 3. a | 3. d | 3. a | 3. d |
| 4. | 4. b | 4. d | 4. d | 4. a |
| 5. b | 5. d | 5. d | 5. b | 5. b |
| 6. d | 6. c | 6. b | 6. b | 6. b |
| 7. d | 7. b | 7. a | 7. a | 7. d |
| 8. b | 8. b | 8. a | 8. b | 8. a |
| 9. a | 9. d | 9. d | 9. c | 9. |
| 10. a | 10. a | 10. b | 10. a | 10. b |
| 11. c | 11. c | 11. c | 11. c | 11. c |
| 12. b | 12. d | 12. b | 12. b | 12. d |
| 13. a | 13. b | 13. c | 13. a | 13. c |
| 14. c | 14. c | 14. c | 14. c | 14. |
| 15. d | 15. d | 15. a | 15. c | 15. |
| 16. d | 16. c | 16. d | 16. c | 16. d |
| 17. c | 17. c | 17. b | 17. d | 17. a |
| 18. c | 18. d | 18. a | 18. d | 18. a |
| 19. a | 19. d | 19. b | 19. c | 19. d |
| 20. | 20. | 20. | 20. | 20. |

<table>
<tr><td>

**Test 11**
1. d
2. d
3. d
4. b
5. a
6. c
7. d
8. a
9. a
10. c
11. c
12. d
13. d
14. c
15. c
16. c
17. a
18. b
19. d
20.

</td><td>

**Test 12**
1. a
2. d
3. b
4. b
5. c
6. d
7. c
8. b
9. d
10. a
11. c
12. d
13. a
14.
15. c
16. d
17. b
18. b
19. d
20.

</td><td>

**Test 13**
1. d
2. d
3. d
4. a
5. b
6. a
7. c
8. a
9. c
10. c
11. c
12. d
13. d
14. d
15. c
16. c
17. d
18. c
19. a
20.

</td><td>

**Test 14**
1. d
2. c
3. b
4. a
5. b
6. d
7. c
8. d
9. c
10. c
11. c
12. b
13. d
14. c
15. d
16. d
17. c
18. c
19. c
20.

</td><td>

**Test 15**
1. a
2. a
3. a
4. a
5. a
6. a
7. b
8. b
9. d
10. c
11. c
12. d
13. b
14. c
15. d
16. c
17. b
18. c
19. b
20.

</td></tr>
<tr><td>

**Test 16**
1. b
2. c
3. a
4. a
5. c
6. b
7. b
8. a
9. b
10. c
11. c
12. b
13. c
14. d
15. d
16. d
17. b
18. b
19. b
20.

</td><td>

**Test 17**
1. b
2. c
3. d
4. b
5. a
6. b
7. b
8. a
9. a
10. c
11. c
12. b
13. c
14.
15.
16. d
17. d
18. b
19. a
20.

</td><td>

**Test 18**
1. d
2. c
3. a
4. b
5. b
6. b
7. c
8. b
9. a
10. c
11. c
12. b
13. a
14.
15. a
16. c
17. c
18. a
19. c
20.

</td><td>

**Test 19**
1. d
2. c
3. d
4. b
5. a
6. c
7. a
8. a
9. d
10. b
11. c
12. d
13. d
14.
15.
16. c
17. a
18. a
19. b
20.

</td><td>

**Test 20**
1. a
2. d
3. b
4. b
5. d
6. b
7. c
8. d
9.
10. b
11. c
12. d
13. d
14. d
15.
16. d
17. a
18.
19. d
20.

</td></tr>
</table>

# Definitions

**abruptly:** suddenly.

**accelerate:** speed up.

**accompanied:** going along with. The blind <u>man</u> was accompanied by a seeing-eye dog.

**adjusting:** fixing. The brakes need adjusting.

**adversely affects:** changes in a bad way. "The use of drugs adversely affects your driving" means that alcohol makes you a dangerous driver.

**alert:** to warn or be on the watch for.

**alcohol:** any drink such as beer, wine, or hard liquor.

**ambulance:** emergency vehicle.

**anticipate:** to look ahead. To anticipate errors of others means to look ahead to mistakes before they are made.

**approach:** to come near.

**beam:** a ray of light. Low beam means the ray of light is close to the road.

**blowout:** the bursting of a tire.

**caution:** being very careful. "Proceed with caution" means to go very carefully.

**convicted:** proven guilty.

**crest:** top of a hill.

**crosswalk:** lines painted across a road to show where people may cross.

**cruising speed:** normal speed. The cruising speed on a superhighway is about 55 mph.

**curve:** a bend in the road.

**decelerate:** slow down.

**defensive driving:** looking out for the other drivers.

**defines:** shows or points out. A single, broken, white line defines traffic lanes. It shows where the lanes are.

**destination:** the place towards which someone is traveling.

**diagonal line:** a line that runs on a slant.

**diamond-shaped:** 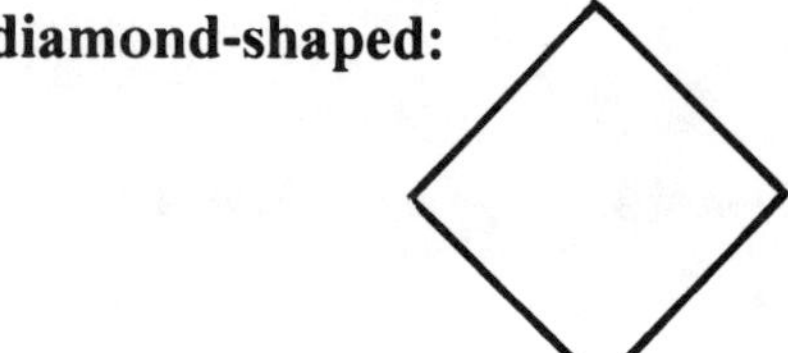

**discharge:** let off. To discharge passengers means to let passengers out of a vehicle.

**drowsy:** sleepy. If you get drowsy while driving, you should rest.

**ease-up:** let up. Ease-up on the gas means to let up or give the car less gas.

**effectively:** to do something as well with less wasted effort.

**emergency:** a time of great danger.

**error:** mistake.

**expect:** look for, or plan for and be ready. Expect, or look for, the other driver to do the wrong thing.

**expressway:** a super-highway.

**fatigue:** being very tired.

**hazardous:** dangerous.

**highway:** a road that is not a city street.

**immediately:** right away.

**impair:** weaken. "Alcohol impairs your vision" means that alcohol weakens your sight.

**intention:** what you plan to do. When you signal your intention to turn, you are telling other drivers that you are going to turn.

**interfere:** get in the way. You can cross a broken, white line if it will not interfere with traffic.

**interrupt:** make a break in.

**intersection:** where two or more streets or roads cross or meet.

**intoxicated:** drunk.

**involved:** to be part of or to be in. "Involved in an accident" means to be in an accident.

**lane:** a strip of road used for a single lane of traffic. A four-lane highway has four strips.

**licensed driver:** a person who has a driver's license.

**maximum:** the highest. "Maximum speed 55" means that 55 mph is the fastest you can go.

**merchandise:** packages, things you buy.

**merging:** to come together. The two lanes of traffic merged into one.

**metallic:** made of metal.

**minimum:** the lowest. "Minimum speed 35" means that 35 mph is the slowest you can go.

**mph:** miles per hour.

**narrower:** less wide. Diagonal lines indicate the road is becoming narrower.

**obstructing:** getting in the way of.

**officer:** a policeman.

**oncoming:** coming toward you, such as oncoming traffic. Walk facing the oncoming traffic.

**opposing:** opposite; coming from the other way.

**ordinary:** regular or usual. Ordinary driving is the kind of driving a person does every day.

**passengers:** people other than the driver who are riding in a vehicle.

**pavement:** the road itself.

**pedestrian:** a person walking.

**penalty:** punishment.

**permits:** allows. When traffic permits, you should move out of the passing lane and into the right lane.

**personal injury:** injury of a person.

**posted:** told by a sign. The speed limit posted is 40 mph.

**precautions:** actions taken to be safe. Wearing a seat belt is a good precaution.

**preparing:** getting ready. He is preparing to turn left.

**prevents:** keeps from taking place. Heavy traffic may prevent you from turning.

**privilege:** a right. He has the privilege of going first.

**proceed:** go on or ahead. When the light turns green, you may proceed.

**prohibit:** to forbid or not allow.

**property damage:** damage to a thing, such as a car.

**receive:** to take on. To receive passengers means to take on passengers in the vehicle.

**rectangular:**

**reduce:** make less or decrease. The amount we see at night is greatly reduced.

**regulate:** to control. Regulatory signs control traffic by telling what the rules are.

**responsible:** to have a duty.

**revoked:** taken away. A person convicted of driving while intoxicated will have his license revoked.

**scene:** place.

**scene of the accident:** where the accident took place.

**separate:** divide.

**signal:** let other drivers know what you are going to do. You can use hand or turn signals.

**single:** one. A single, broken line is one line.

**shoulder:** the side of the road, along the edge of the pavement.

**slippery:** easy to slip or skid on.

**square:**

**stop line:** a white line painted across the pavement to show where vehicles must stop before traffic signs or signals.

**surface:** top layer.

**suspended:** taken away for a time and then given back. His license was suspended for six months.

**swerve:** to turn suddenly. If you drive when you are drowsy, your car may swerve off the road.

**symbol:** a simple picture that stands for something.

**temporarily:** for a very short time.

**traffic:** vehicles moving along.

**traffic control device:** a traffic light.

**triangle:**

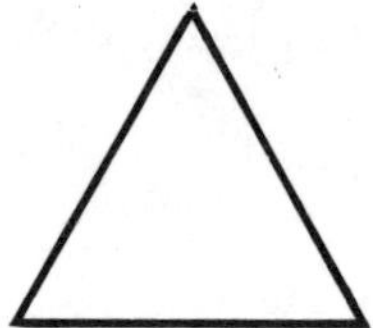

**U-turn:** a full turn that puts you going in the opposite direction on the same road.

**vehicle:** a car, truck, bus, or motorcycle.

**vibrate:** shake.

**vision:** sight.

**yield:** to give up a right; to give up the right-of-way. You must yield the right-of-way to a police car.
A YIELD sign is a down-pointed triangle.

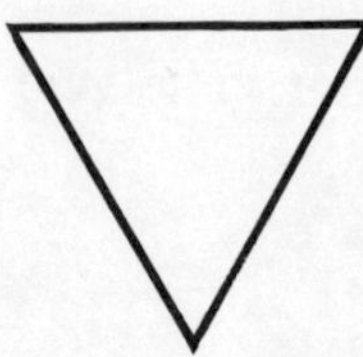